Reflections in Time

An Anthology of Poetry

Edited By Amanda Read

δ

Published by Dogma Publications

Dogma Publications 3 Fulmar Lane Wellingborough
Northants NN8 4AE England

Reflections in Time

Anthology Collection © Amanda Read 2004
Copyright © Dogma Publications and Individual Contributors

Cover picture taken from Willem van Aelst's
Vase of Flowers with Watch
1656
Staatliche Museen, Kassel

All Rights Reserved

First Published 2004
by Dogma Publications

ISBN 1-84591-001-X

Printed in Great Britain for Dogma Publications

Reflections in Time

Contents

Contents continued

Contents continued

Carefree

Let me remember how it used to be
Playing in fields called home for tea
Our mothers voice could reach out far & wide
Bringing us all home back to her side
Summer days always seemed so long
If I remember each winter snow came along
I recollect how yucky others getting kissed
And a chance of skipping school was never to be missed
Our future plans included Knights and princesses
Not working nights and paying our taxes
Care free abandon I miss so much
When the worst of the day was the egg sandwich you got
But what I miss most seems to be
The way my mum and dad were to me
There is a changing point in life
When roles reverse almost overnight
Once we were fed and watered washed and cleaned
Now it's changed it's them that has these needs
When I'm am old my children will also see
That exactly the same will happen to me
So many things have had to change
Yet so few faces have stayed the same.

Sarah Spratt

A Shattered Mind

A shattered mind
A broken soul
A never ending falling hole
To whom I have to scream my name
A dark thought to push the blame
A breeding bond of last pretence
To what will come to my defence
A bleak existence all of my own
I shall wilt here all alone
Nothing brought
Nothing beared
Nothing had and nothing shared
Never will my thoughts prevail
Can I ever leave a trail?

Jenni West

Now He's Gone

Standing by me through sunshine and storm,
He was my angel, my heart and my home.
But then all of a sudden he fell asleep,
And left me to hurt, to cry and to weep.

I felt so confused, so lonely and scared,
I wish he knew how much I cared.
His memories hurt and make me cry
He went so quickly, with no goodbye.

He was so loving, so gentle and kind.
He was the love that's hard to find.
He soothed my heart with his gentle touch,
Now I'm in pain, I miss him so much.

He worked so hard and he was the best,
But he had to leave us so he could rest.
He'll always stay within my heart
Though far away but never apart...

Nargas Abdullah

Hold Onto Your Dreams

Hold onto your dreams even when times are blue,
  When all your hope has run askew.
  When times are tough and the winds of change
Have been left astray,
  Don't let those dreams fade away.

Hold onto your dreams firmly with both hands,
  Never let go even when the heart demands.
  These dreams are the start of your destiny,
A link to God from all your sinful humanity.

Hold onto your dreams even if upon the edge,
  Cast aside your possessions over the ledge.
Fly into the skies with the power of freedom
  To unite the people of this Kingdom.

Sheila Cheng

Why?

There in the darkness appears a moon,
I love to look out of the window in my bedroom,
How peaceful and calm it is at night,
Just think a few hours later there will be light,
Days become weeks, weeks becomes years,
Throughout these times is doubt and fears,
Why is there hatred in this life?
Whether it be abroad, the universe or fife,
Life is such a trying time,
When you have to lay it all on the line,
Life changes fast all around us a time goes by,
When all said and done I let out an almighty sigh,
Why do people want to kill others
And shorten the life that they may have had?
Then the family suffer and they lose
Someone close and they are sad,
Life has a weird phase of images,
There's life on the planet and the dead in the cemeteries,
Why are we born to die?
And all the mysteries are left unknown and the questions why?

Nora Colston

Remember

Remember when our lives were still entwined?
Our love was like the fruit upon a seasoned, sun kissed vine.
Our days were numbered then...
Do you still remember when
You loved me and I loved you,
And we sailed across
A sea of never-ending blue...
And I loved you?

Sophie Morton

Coma

In the darkening of the night
That girl was snatched from out of sight
Out of sight but not of mind
To that girl we'll never find.
All I can do is sit and wait,
I love you but it's too late,
I'll sit by you and hold your hand,
And watch you slip through like sand.

Louisa Aizlewood

Autumn

The simple pleasure of raking leaves
Whilst thinking thoughts that often deceives
Putting the summer to memory's test
Almost sure that it was the best
Childhood goes with the summer, too
And memories like leaves are raked for the flu
All wind and weather and living and going
Far from a time of early sowing
Til another spring and another birth
Will measure us all for what we are worth.

Maurice Bagley

Warrior

Craft of beauty washes over the waves
Taking us to unspoilt caves
Copper mines private beaches
Warrior will drift your mind away
Weekends spent in some great place
Laughing and joking along the way
Serious talks late at night
Shallow water's she wont like
Craft of beauty washes over the waves
Days and weeks drift into years
As we cross those blue waves
Peace and quiet this is our life
Alone at last just the two of us.

Paul Harvey

Despair

Those contorted faces depicted-
Even soundless one knows
Their cries are not human
But animal, drawn from their depths.
Is there no possible cessation
Of this endless horror film?
The daily toll of bombs and guns,
Missiles sneaking from a distance...
Is the new architecture all jagged gaps,
Pot holed roads, leaking sewage,
Miserable existence in surviving corners?
Is the world filled with ragged children,
Eyes enormous in aged faces,
Bellies a mockery of fullness?
With increasing frustration we see
Leaders with false bonhomie
Smile-masked faces, endlessly talking,
Endlessly travelling-for what?
Where does one excise the inborn hatreds
The martyrdoms, lost generations?
Centuries of culture lost in present 'history;.
Is the world spinning out of control?
God knows!

Di Bagshawe

As She Lay Next To Me

Awoken by fate, a love so sublime,
Consumed by your beauty, you lay next to me,
My senses intoxicated, your scent so divine,
As I breath in your soul, entwined, we become two.
A shaft of stray sunlight, touches your shoulder,
Warming soft skin, so smooth to embrace,
A face full of kindness, now silent in dreams,
Eyes of pure passion, hidden to sight.
Lips soft and tender, I long to caress,
Hair of pure velvet, that shimmers with life,
Your voice floating softly, cradled hushed in the air,
Full of contentment, while love steals our hearts.

Together to suffer, the stress and the pain,
To hold in my arms, protecting from fear,
Devotion unrivalled, no temptation to stray,
The world spinning past us, yet our love still remains.
Intimate moments, an open fire, fine wine,
Care, love and passion, imbuing our minds,
Burns deep inside, to be forged in our care,
As we step on the path, life lays before us,
Are we to marry? Do you carry our child?
Grow old together? I cannot say,
All I know as for now, is that I wish I could capture,
This perfect moment together, as you lay next to me.

Peter Morris-Webb

Riverside Parting

The murmuring hills are drowned
In shards of moonlight;
White in the moon-flame, are the wild, dim waters
Of the mist veiled river.
The rippling waves awaken to my sorrow
As my grief cries loud.

Where will my dreaming soul tonight be found?
Will she sink into the stillness
Of the Midnight song?
Then linger silently beneath
The withering sedges
That whispers your name
Only to fade when the dawn light
Beckons the sky,
Through the white pearls of rain.

The riverside willow hangs low
Across your drifting boat;
With howling winds
Her branches entwine the oars
Your hands unfold
Their fleeting embrace.
Turning your head,
You see my tears
The moon mirrored in my eyes.
A lone hawk hovers
As silence reigns.

In vain, the river soars to the night sky,
Thundering faintly beyond the lotus pools
Inch by inch my heart is consumed
As you drift beneath the glinting stars.

Nilofar Hossain

A Precious Moment

When I first saw his gentle face
And hair of purest gold
Without a shadow of a doubt
My Lord, I did behold
He stood so closely to me
That I called to him aloud
Oh Jesus, Oh Jesus I adore thee
But he did not make a sound.

His smile was like a warm caress
That I fell down to my knees
Just giving praise unto this man
Who gave His life for me
I hardly dared to blink mine eyes
In case He disappear
I might not get another chance
To have my Lord so near
He left as swiftly as he came
And in that empty space
I pray I'll find it filled again
With that radiant Godly face.

George W Baxter

Cages

Caged birds sing their dreams to life,
unhindered by the bars across the sky
that is so much more than free within
each tiny breast that bursts with golden sun.

The birds are not their cages
and I am more than flesh and mind,
more than a prisoner of your need
to tie an angel to your back
as you search for love among the thorns,
never daring to look up or lose control,
frightened that your sense of free
might urge you to surrender
to the truth of your own wings and fly.

So I will dance our dreams to life,
the chains that we have wrapped around
my waist for fear you lose your angel,
and your way, are not as real as the love
that lives inside our hearts of golden sun.

Shell Heller

The Grieving Hours Of Early Morning

Morning was born prematurely that day,
Thrust into a foreign world
Screaming and gasping for air.
The sun did not rise as high as usual
And was subdued,
As you were in your final hours,
By the clouds
As they processed across the sky,
Their march hurried along by the wind
Which seemed to echo your memory.
The rain fell much more poignantly,
A substitute for the tears I was incapable of shedding.
The leaves fell to their graves,
Twisting and turning in the breeze,
Their journeys prolonged in a desperate attempt to remain alive.
It is in the grieving hours of the early morning,
When the air is cool whilst the colours warm,
That I remember you most;
And yet as the wind brushes my cheek,
The way you used to,
I am pained to admit that I cannot remember what you looked like.
You exist only as a memory,
A feeling,
A familiar sound,
A significant place.
And, as I sit staring at the leaves on the ground,
I search within their montage of colours
In the vain attempt I might see a portrait of your face.

Joanna Bayley

Dark Touch

Icy fingers chilling my spine
Eyes watching from the corners of my mind
Black alleyways haunting my dreams
Luminous faces that I've never seen.

Quiet footsteps outside my door
The voices calling creeping and crawling
Singing their black lullaby
Leading me into the shadows.

Black silhouettes whispering darkly
Hidden with secrets and tales untold
Hiding away while their pasts unfold.

Locked away in the most secret of places
Places nobody can see
The deep dark chambers of the taunting mind
The lost corners that no one can find.

Victoria Cookson

Société Anonyme

Thought and Chance sat drinking
cheap wine together
in a Parisian café
late into the night
pondering Mallarmé's statement
that 'Chance will always triumph
over Thought'.

Said Chance to Thought
'If you were as lucky as me
then you wouldn't need to think
at all'
Said Thought to Chance
'Chance, my friend,
would be a fine thing'
and laughing
they stumbled off
into the early hours of the morning
passing unheeded their sister Fate
as she lay
weaving a pernicious spell
beneath the arches of a church.

Paul Bett

Although

Although writing to persons unknown
is uncomfortable

like tube socks in too tight trainers

and as unfamiliar
as sliding into someone else's car to drive
(the seat sloped back too far and
too close to the steering wheel)

sometimes
there's a link

(two-baked-bean-cans-tied-together-with-knotted-string)

and it spans oceans.

Christopher Waugh

I Solved The World's Problems

I solved the world's problems
Sitting at my café table.
I emptied the sugar bowl
And stacked the cubes into armies-
Half to my left, and half to my right.
Taking a brown cube and a white cube
I stirred the two into my cup of tea,
And sipped the sweetened, sugary brew.
I'll be honest, I couldn't taste the
Difference and reckoned there might
Be some wisdom there swilling around
Under the guidance of the spoon.
They look so different but taste much the same.
The café, I noticed was filled with a mix
Of beautiful people, of all races
Each stirring their morning cuppas.
Lord, I'm not sure how many sugars you take,
But the kettle's on!

Curtis Tappenden

Days Of Living

In age you have reached the Zenith,
Yet, still to unfold, those tales of Ypres
Then, to be no time for weeps,
However much it is put behind
It ever stays fresh in the mind.
The memory plays many tricks
As time passes by and the clock ticks,
You can speak of beauty abound
As, the south coast, you wander around.
Now happier stories of which to boast
Swans to fee, with breakfast toast.
Still the channel stretching for miles
Brings back, quite a few smiles
When those many friends you meet
Always fresh, the memories of Ypres,
The strong bonds you have made
Lasted to this day, a decade.

Edith Blagrove

Row

Completely out of control, mad and psychotic.
Hysterical crying and screams of stress -
inability to reason or rationalise,
complete lack of empathy,
meaningless words flung from person to person.
Crazy and disturbing, fear, insecurity and helplessness.
Reckless anger and absence of love, care, understanding.

Centre of the conflict,
object of scorn
yet innocent of hatred.

Empty and aching,
alone and without confidante.
An already painful heart ripped and gashed by cruel accusations.

Why all this conflict, this change?
Why no security of love, no peace?
Nobody left, only frames of people who once were...
no soul, no concern - just self-absorption.

Megan Brand

In Awe Of Edgar A Poe

The dream, the dream 'tis here again...
Slivered flesh I fantasise of in my darkest dreams,
A human stew or broth of you
My tasty one; now sleeping got.
'Tis time to make my broth for maw and gulf,
To tender you before the *rigor mortis* takes its toll
I fillet your heart slowly over pot of heathen brew
And as the slices drop so thickly into bloody stew,
A single smile, a hint of guile upon my drooling lips;
Your entrails on the kitchen floor
I'll feed your black cat with and more,
But I shall have the lions share
Laugh at me now; they would not dare.
Thrice I stir the bubbling brew
'Tis time to take the plunge in you
At first my love just a sip or two,
I place the spoon betwixt my moistened lips and...
You have such subtle flavour, which I alone now savour.

Stephen Michael McGowan

Destiny

I led my tribe through the Dawn of Time
Over dense marshlands, crossing dusty plains
With bows on backs and spears to hand
We the first hunters, from a race called man.

We followed no path, yet wandered far
The creator was praised with ritual fire
Braves killed the demons that plundered our people
Women looked to the skies, for a sign of grace.

The mountain spitting fire, offered us no harm
Rivers running wide, could not divide my people
Wild ponies we caught, so rode into fame
The Tribesmen of America was our common name.

It was over the buffalo herds our nation fought
Many braves in agony died, few survived
As over barren ground our armies sped
Much Human blood over the earth was shed.

I was with my tribe as we crossed the ridge
An unmarked line where dwells the Divine
Garbed in paint for making war
These were the last clothes that I ever wore.

I led my tribe to a home in Heaven high
Rivers running wide...Plains bare and dry
Phantoms, huge, red-eyed...eerie cries
Even Death could not divide my people.

George Bremer

Green Turns To Yellow

It was the daylight that woke me as I laid upon my bed,
By an open door, 'Good morning!' a familiar voice then said,
A tired yawn, an aching stretch, the beginning of the day,
And green had turned to yellow, in a certain kind of way.

A short walk down the corridor, it was recess time again,
To the dining hall and breakfast-each Tuesday's just the same.
The neatly planted flowerbeds we pass along the way,
And green had turned to yellow, in a certain kind of way.

Then it's off to work, via the gate-they look inside your bag,
The laboured walk and heavy eyes, some gasping on a fag!
Past the textile works and footwear, where rolls of cloth just lay,
Where the green had turned to yellow, in a certain kind of way.

Find your place and dust your chair, your work has just begun,
All boxes full of finished goods to get the order done,
'Tomorrow we're on something new,' I heard the Guv'nor say,
'The green will turn to yellow'-in a certain kind of way!

At half past four the siren blows to free us from our work,
All the evening is our free time-for us to enjoy a perk!
But the light is fading quickly as autumn's here to stay,
And the greens have turned to yellow, in a certain kind of way.

And so it is, a year goes by; it's gone before we know,
The final rattling of the keys and then it's time to go,
And as I make that one last walk I can turn my head and say:
'That green has turned to yellow-in a certain kind of way!'

Robert Brooker

The Candle

Blue, lilac, yellow
Even a glimmer of orange
Wick, wax, sweet aroma
Dancing brightly
In front of me
I sit here a while
Watching it flicker
Enjoying the silence
On this peaceful night
As I look through
That agile flame
Snapshots of memory
Flash through my mind
Piercing it with laughter
Painting it with smiles
Tainting it with sadness
The flame dies
Burns the candle out
The faint flickers
Of remembrance
Fade into the darkness.

Laura Lamarca

Life

A final warning arrives in the post,
A default for missing a loan repayment,
A ringing phone executes the silence,
'Have you considered a credit card?'
More people to owe a days work to...so this is it, this is life?

I'm going to be late for work again,
Shouldn't have chilled out in the shower,
I've been warned about this before,
"Do you know if my taxi will arrive soon?"
Bet it won't show up at all...so this is it, this is life?

A friend was shot down last night,
suppose he had it coming to him,
said the wrong thing to the wrong lad,
"But what does a young man know?"
Doesn't know when to shut up it seems...so this is it, this is life?

Can't find a mouthful in the bins,
Bastard rich people haven't left a scrap,
normally throw half a meal away,
"Suppose there's still tea time to come!"
Unless they're full after this feast...so this is it, this is life...

It shouldn't be like this, this shouldn't be life.

Jimi Capewell

The Lassies

A lang time ago, lassies taen they love potions,
Noo, wi' papers and tele', we have ither notions,
We buy fae the druggiest a motley collection
I'm shair in his windae you'e seen the selection,
There's cream for yer hands, and cream for yer face,
The cream fae the coo, jist puts fat the wrong place,
There's stuff for your een, lang eyelashes too,
Wi' colours that range fae white tae sky blue,
Paint for your fingers, taes tae if ye care,
An for any young lass that's gey thin o' the hair,
A wig is the answer, red, black, straight or curly,
Fell dear hae nae doobt, just dig deep in yer purlie,
There's lotions that turn ye fae white intae broon;
They'll introduce silver when we land on the moon,
Stuff for yer oxters, tae make ye smell sweet,
Pads for your bunions, to ease yer puir feet.
Oil for your bath, and rouge for yer dimples
Face packs made o' mud, tae get rid o' yer pimples.
Scents o' a kinds tae mak yer lad pant,
Peels tae reduce ye, and mak yer flesh scant,
A' colours o' lipsticks wi' strange sounding names,
Some mak ye look bloodless an' suffering pains,
Nae wonder we woman are tired all the time,
It taks endless patience tae mak us look fine,
So a word to you men, afore ye fent in a heap,
Remember that beauty is only skin deep.

Anne M Gibson

What Colour Is The Sky In Your World?

I want to scream and shout at the whole lot of you!
But what's the point when the things have already been said.
It hurts me when I see you hurt others,
And there's nothing I can do...
When nobody can do anything.
I look at you and see nothing but guilt,
In denial, weak, cover ups and hate!
You call yourself grown?
I have little respect for you...
Actually I have no respect for you.
Do me a favour and please tell me
What colour is the sky in your world?
I have grown up myself; I've been hurt;
I've cried I have known shame.
But I must say I'm happy,
I'm proud of myself...
I know what colour the sky is in my world its blue,
But yours I don't have a clue.
People like you will die unhappy and miserable...
You know why?
Because your PRIDE and your attitude STINKS.
You walk over people who you are supposed to love...you hurt them.
Because of you pride and attitude
Everyone has turned their back on you.
Now tell me what colour is the sky in your world?

Mellissa Brown

Grandad

I remember the old man when I was a child
His sparkling eyes told a thousand stories
Each line on his face read like a book
Tales of love and battles filled with glory.

When I was with him, a game would begin
Always laughing and playing around
I felt like the centre of his earth
A better friend could never be found.

As I grew older the bond became strong
His stories taught me to be good
Life had dealt him a pretty tough hand
I'd earn his respect, make him proud if I could.

Now he is gone, an empty space fills my heart
I miss him and at times I feel low
I know he is watching and loving me still
He will always be there in my soul.

Sally Robin Monks

Dreams

So long I have wished for thoughts of night
to merge within the morning light,
For not to sleep to see my dreams
to live my life no thoughts unseen,
For all the heart and soul I hold
to join my life and make so bold,
The summer sun to last all day
to keep the dark of night at bay,
All this and more in my mind I see
tired of dreams long for reality.

Duncan Bryant

Surrender

When the sun surrenders the daytime,
And the moon surrenders the night,
That's when our minds are a lifetime,
And we dance in the realm of the light.

When only our hearts go on beating,
And we wake to humble the day,
It's then that our love is repeating,
Those wonders which here with us stay.

Ourselves are but just a reflection,
Of rhythm and time here alone,
When light and the dark in perfection,
Retreat like a bird that has flown.

Robin Castell

31

Your Soul

Your soul forever burns this life
Toxic fumes of your delight
Pain and torture bring your fear
And death begins to creep so near
A shadow cast upon the floor
A face of evil at your door
The look that falls upon your face
Now fills the same demonic place
The one that lingers in your heart
The one that drove you to this start
The very place that held your fear
For that ever lasting year.

Danny Cave

My Tree

As Winter winds approach and blind
Remember me I once was kind
My leaves attracted you to me
Your love was given without a fee.

But now my branches all lay bare
My disguise removed without a care
Branches reach but never find
The love that once was in your mind.

Abandon me no warmth to share
Before Winter snows fall from the air
I once was bright you loved me more
A shining light on a darkened shore.

Like seasons changes my life with you
Summer, Spring and Autumn too
Then Winter fell the hardest one
Your coats too thin to keep us warm.

Your so called love is spent and worn
The winds will bend me just like corn
I remember but only just
That love proclaimed, was only lust.

Mark Ritchie

Dirty Pretty People

All you pretty people
looking in the mirror
vanity isn't the only mistake you are making
beautify my mind
it isn't in the eye of the beholder
its in my hands
around your neck dirty private church
dirty little steeple
dirty broken mirrors
they're dirty pretty people.

Heroin Fuelled Wings.
And all because the feeling
Of that metal on my skin is old
And Step by step
you break the glass floor of my emotion
A personal f**k you.

Take my hand
And lead me
To my cocoon
Emerge as something else
Self indulgence
Is the key to light relief
A bottled feeling
In this sea of smiles.

Sam Cole

Were We So Bad Then?

If we smashed someone's window
They would always seek us out!
Grounded by mum and the belt off dad
We'd be known as a 'right little lout!'

If we dared to answer back
Teachers gave us a thump!
A neighbour would run after us
A good-hiding on our rump!

Sit at home nearly every night?…no,
We were told to 'get out and play!'
One of the scariest games of all
Was to knock on doors and run away!

Mugging someone for their cash
It just never entered out heads.
If we had nowt it stayed like that
We had homes, were clean and got fed!

Cycle on the footpath
Grown-ups would order us off.
Most of them knew our mothers
And at home we'd fear that knock!

Raiding an orchard was risky
The owners would give chase.
Apples we nicked, made us ill
And were very bitter to taste!

Some of us had a sly ciggy
Behind the bike sheds at school.
Woe betide us on getting caught
Punishments made us feel cool!

Clifford Chambers

35

True Love

A special time has come to celebrate
A life together brought about by fate
You both sailed across the ocean wide
To find each other and forever to abide.

Your thoughts travel down memory lane
Of highs and lows, the joy and pain
Of first love when you soared to dizzy heights
The doubts, the confusion, and the sleepless nights.

The passionate love that ended each day
And sent you spiralling as high as the Milky Way
Bonding you together until you have became one
Filling you with love that would never be undone.

The day you made your solemn promise
With true love that was sealed with a kiss
You exchanged golden rings and became man and wife
And began your journey down the road of life.

In your hearts there is always Spring
As free as the swallow on the wing
Your love is as infinite as the stars above
You have been blessed with everlasting love.

There was caring love, forever constant
A sharing love for your longed for infant
A comforting love to allay your fears
A gentle love through the Autumn years.

And now you have reached your Golden Year
I will toast you with a glass of cheer
And wish you happiness as you travel on
Through a healthy life that will remain ever strong.

Phillis Green

Fade To Black

When I heard that you were dead
I couldn't understand how
when the Earth's mantle shattered where you fell
that the spider cracks didn't reach my feet fifty miles away.

I stared and stared but there was no sign of the earthquake.

I thought my hearing must have failed
because I couldn't hear the streets
all around you ripping themselves to pieces
or the screams of your loved ones on the other side of town

I put down the phone and through the window
a traffic jam of rush-hour red snaked away through the city
'Why haven't they stopped?' I thought 'haven't they heard?'

I guess you never found a way to split the atom after all.

Alison Sarah Charlton

Caught

I'm caught in your web
and I can't break free.
I feel like your eating
up inside of me.
You are a spider
consuming your prey
I'm the fly
I can't get away.
I'm caught in your web
I can't believe it is true
now you're spinning
another
but I still love you.

Dawn Coser

Change

The Autumn gold sinks sullen into grey.
Black night becomes much longer than the day.
Autumn rain corrupts dead leaves to mould.
Time stumbles, slowing down, and all seems old.

Where is Winter? Where is the cleansing frost,
By which all this grey dampness can be lost?
One year divided cleanly from the last,
Leaving that year's sorrows to the past.

Now comes sharp frost, silently by night,
Painting green fields and hedges glittering white,
Branches turn to fairy wands as if for fun,
Sheep glisten pink like sugared mice in early sun.

And with that early sun - blue cloudless skies,
Crude countryside the brightness dignifies.
Nature's myriad eyes now close in sleep,
There's promises for next year they must keep.

Bob Crossley

Salisbury Cathedral In Summer

The tall spire stands
Silently on plain.
Proffer, a gathering of
Clouds just drifting by.
Magically, the sunlight
Triumphantly gleams on
Cathedral rooftop.
To set you eyes upon.

As you stroll across the luscious
Green meadows grass
How the time quickly passes
As you move in with the
Swans obtrusively-
Ones at risk.

Gently roam to the back of cathedral close.
And see the cloisters with many pages
Of history always to see the spirit of
Faith has never faded through ages.
To be here, a feeling of spiritual
Refreshment to the visitor be ecclesiastical.

"Sammy" Michael Davis

The Proud Scot
(Dedicated to my father J R G Sinclair 03.04.31 – 22.11.03)

A proud Scot lies in tatters,
  Esteem breached by cell attack,
Disease now rapidly spreading
  Body wide, like books in a library rack.

A proud Scot lies in tatters,
  Once strong but now too weak
In his physical body, his mind still sharp,
  His spiritual soul he now doth seek.

A proud Scot lies in tatters,
  Help gleaned from angels above,
From god and the powers that surround him,
  In their presence he fits like a hand in a glove.

A proud Scot lies in tatters,
  Goodbye earth as he rises towards
A new life, a white light heavily littered with love;
  "Welcome Home" is the sign on Gods heavenly doors.

Home at last...

A proud Scot once lay in tatters.
  Now spiritually alive amongst family and friends
No more sickness, discomfort, or unbearable pain
  A new force awakens with known spiritual trends.

Alison Sinclair

Dreamer

I stand and gaze upon your smile,
a deep reflection held in my soul as a child.
To grow within the warmth of love,
long forgotten, tears flood your eyes in a moment.
Dreamer. I became as one within you,
to lose you far away.

I stay inside your heaven now
no longer lonely once more I'm safe in your arms.
To feel your touch across my mind,
fills me only, full of desire for my being.
Dreamer. Really all that needs a meaning.
To feel us fade away.

For you, suns will never set
I will not, forget promises we made.
Somewhere there's a harbour though we pass her by,
where our ships can be and safely lie.
In the warmth of her arms,
inside a perfect day.
And with each passing moment…we wait to sail away.

Alan Rowley

The Ministering Angel

Are you a ministering angel
Sent from the highest throne?
The celestial messenger to me
Is manifest in flesh and bone.
Gentleness from you flows
As, within your arms, I am enclosed.

There are no external wings
Or robes of dazzling white
That herald the glad news you bring
Of succour and delight.
You have come in human form
And, to my frail flesh, have conformed.

You are my saviour
In this overwhelming sea of stress-
You provide a secure harbour.
My sanctuary is in your embrace.
The storm your open arms will quall
For nought will penetrate your divine walls.

Your heavenly aura is exuded
And charity you enact
As you reveal your sanctified nature
When we were enjoined in that sacred pact-
The eternal nature of our union
Transcends all boundaries of time.

Andrew Drury

The Question Of Spring

Is it true that spring is here?
Is it really as it seems,
Or one of nature's heavenly dreams?

Has winter shed it's overcoat?
Do you know for certain
That spring's drawn back its curtain?

Can I truly be convinced
When I awake, it's light at dawn
And bulbs are flowering on the lawn?

Do you know the answer please?
Has spring really come at last and winter settled in the past?

Yes! I believe it could be true.
Have you received an inner sign,
Or is this joyful glow just mine?

My heart and soul say 'Yes, it's true'.
But can you give a special reason
Why God has sent this perfect season?

Ann Cecilia Dugdale

Poverty Seems To Stay

My eyes seem to fail all the while
I am old but poverty makes me as small as a child.
My diets are limited and I am weak
Many are they that said 'Blessed are the meek'.
However, only a few have washed my feet
And none reach out and gave me meat.
Poverty! Poverty! Poverty is all I always have
Poverty just seems to stay!
Oh! Cruel! Cruel poverty why did you have to come my way?

I tried! Yes, I tried! I tried my very best!
But this condition just doesn't want to give me rest
It holds my hands and sucks my breast
It rents my clothes and rapes me in aggressiveness
I cry out loud, but there was still no pity for me
It just goes on and on and blows my dream and fantasy
Oh! You! You wretched poverty! Why don't you let me go?
Yes, you! You same poverty that always sway my way!
Leave me! Leave me Poverty! Leave me this very day!

Winsome Ebanks

Religion

I feel I'm losing my religion,
Uncomfortable and inconvincible,
Well learned traditions and beliefs,
Mean little to me.
But still I wish I could
Give myself wholly, to belong.
Always though the true individual,
Yet one remains,
I feel it and I am no fool.
Recognizing some mysterious intervene,
Guided by my instinctual values,
I disregard complex rituals,
Develop my own personal mission.
Like missioners gone before,
Helped because I'm loved,
And loved because I'm helping.

Sarah-Rose Finnegan

Moody Feelings

I hate this feeling the mood I am in,
Some days I'm up some I'm down,
It's funny how your life can be turned upside down
I think of the things that happen in the past
I wish these things did not have to last.
Some days I think of doing something silly
But will this do me good no not really.
I talk to my councillor he helps a lot,
But really it should all be forgot.
I try to talk to my Husband but I get upset
I know he can't always answer my request.
I hope some day soon I can be back to myself
Tell every one to get on with things themselves
Until that day I will hope and pray
That I can carry on and say
Hope all this lot will go away.

Ellen Gigg

Sun, Moon And Stars

The sun is...

the centre of a daisy swaying in a gentle summers breeze
a bright new tennis ball as it shoots through the air
a roaring fire burning through the sea.

The moon is...

a slippery white banana boiling in oil
a ball of clouds misted against the blackest sky
a lump of Danish Blue melting above us.

The stars are...

eyes of golden crowns shining down on us
brightly coloured buttons set in to a black coat
a staircase to heaven where all people stroll.

Lucy Grant

Bequia

Did they smell the frangipani
from the hill-top where they sat?
Did they eat the guava fruit
in the time which they had set

to repel all other comers
from this gem of luscious green?
Those interlopers set their guns
at south towards low Mustique,

St. Vincent in the north did
shadow them from harm
kept clear water for their trade
of spice and fruit and man.

Arthur Greenwood

Falling Leaf

The days, the time, nothing to. Me,
Hazel, green, my eyes are blue,
There's no sense, meaningless, do I really smile?
Not down, just looking side ways.
I'm here now I'm here
never there.
Like the moaning leaf escaping its friends,
now drifts to far from home.
What now it whispers with the wind,
What now...what now...what now?
Landed, abandoned, this sure of life.
Found, lifted .in hands of time.
Fate? Freedom? Reality?
Blue, green, my eyes are blind.
The leaf will never know.

Gareth Evans

You Drank Coffee

I thought you were the one for me
You drank coffee, I drank tea.

Sometimes we could laugh and talk
You would cycle, I would walk.

Finding rhythm in everything
You would play, I would sing.

Us together against the rest
You thought you knew, I just guessed.

When the game had been all played
You had left, I had stayed.

Where was it that you had to go?
You owe me something, I should know.

Ellen Jones

My Mistakes

On September 15th,
2003,
I attempted suicide.
With scissors I cut,
Deep into my wrist.
Blood came,
Made to explain.
But I still don't know!

On January 14th,
2004,
I attempted suicide.
With scissors I cut,
Deep into my wrist,
Twenty times.
Did not explain,
Because I don't know!

After a third time,
I stood accused,
As a mental health case.
Was deserted for good.
Why don't I stop?
Because I don't know!

Aled Seago

Autumn

When balmy days of Summer start to fade,
And temperatures drop lower down the scale;
When ghostly mists enshroud both field and glade,
And slowly daylight hours begin to fail;
When sounds of mowing are no longer heard
As Nature slides back gently into rest;
When fiery leaves by gentle breezes stirred
Transform the trees with fiery foliage dressed-
Then with the change of scene fresh days have come
From Summer into colourful Autumn.

H J Griffin

The Rock In The Sea

Where the wind and the sky meet the sea
There my home shall be.
The waves will touch the shore
Near my ever open door.
Of stormy spray or gentle calm
The natural sound will be my balm.
With silvery tint the evening light
Will fade the sea into the night.
I'll be there under stars so bright
Till at dawn across the bay
The sun will greet another day.

Sue Handoll

My Bumblebee

If I were a flower under a big oak tree,
And you were a bumblebee, who came to visit me,
We'd sit and talk the day away,
And watch the clouds roll by,
Until the sun started to slip out of the golden sky,
The time has come for you to go,
So fly away my friend,
And I will stay and watch the stars,
Until the brand new day,
The sun comes up and on the wind,
The sound of beating wings,
My bumblebee comes back to me,
The two of us are friends.

Michael Thorpe

Bangkok

It's times like these I hear the whisper
Of old Nick's passing and his whiskers
a remedy for unwanted giving's
for feisty natives
different living.
A single drag for a companion
A faithful hound
A sweet D'Artagnan
Perhaps the ethers while I'm sleeping
will conspire for the good
of my safekeeping.

Antony Hateley

On A Cold Winter's Night

I stood amongst my friends and brothers,
I knew some names but not the others,
My clothes were thin, I felt the cold,
We'll send winter uniform we were told,
The warmth of a fire we couldn't light,
For fear of revealing all in the night.

Following the whispers down the trenches,
The dead and dying left their stenches,
I tried to sleep, but it wouldn't come,
My rifle poised, on the trigger my thumb,
Did I now stand in the grave that I'd dug?
'Mother' would I call if death did tug?

I took some smokes out of a packet,
Some matches too from my jacket,
Passed them out, kept one for me,
Lit mine first, the enemy now see,
As I passed it on, they go to aim,
He lit it, they fired, I called his name.

Medic I shouted, but it's too late,
The light I gave him was his fate,
I'll never forget, my very best friend,
Mother, I'm sorry, it was me at the end,
A brother and son, we've both now lost,
Freedom we fought for, our lives were the cost.

Kathy Hirons

Why?

My son stands there-alone-so tall
A quiet gentleness Him surrounds
We are apart-alone-forlorn
Our hopes and fears are not unfound
'Why?'
My heart cries out in pain
'Should you suffer so much pain?'
I know they will crucify Him
The only being free from sin
'You were betrayed by one you loved
as decreed by your Father in Heaven above'
'Never once have you ever rebelled
against your allotted task'.
'Why do you so silently stand, undefended?'
I ask
Your words, your thoughts, your every act
Will last the whole world through.
But, at this time and moment
my heart bleeds for you.

Grace Hoggan

Yesterday

Yesterday, was the last day
Of the life game.
I did not win it,
I did not lose it,
I never learnt to play that game.

Today I still wait to see
If by any luck the game will cease
Standing by the wall
Next to the fans
Yelling like them,
Looking like them,
But lost in the mirage of the screaming crowd.

Tomorrow; I see
The skies in disguise.
The sun rising up,
Between the silvery skies.
Through the cracks
I can feel air,
Light a bird in flight
In the land of the living,
Waiting,
Wanting
Dreaming of another life
In an afterlife with life,
Without soul.
Immortality,
Here: on earth.

Ebere Ikerionwu

The Angel

I felt the gentle breeze from an angel's wing
As it brushed against my brow.
And heavenly choirs sang.
A golden glow surrounded it, as I was lifted high.
And I saw my earthly body.
And swiftly passed it by.
The golden glow got stronger as I journeyed on my way.
The angel's wings were gently beating as in its arms I lay.
I know this was not a dream as dreams fade when you wake.
I do believe the angel made a heavenly mistake.
Some day I'll know for certain if that angle lost its way.
Or was it just a vivid dream that didn't fade away.
But as I sit and ponder, it becomes quite crystal clear.
I was given another chance.
   That's why I'm still here.

Bernard Holliman

St. Andrew's Day
(The Awakening)

A new dawn beckons the nation
The future in our hands,
Let us arise, renewed in mind and deed,
To strive and build a great creation
A new beginning in our lands,
To keep the good, to till, the new to seed.

With care, Scotia nurtures the new
To flower, inspire and aid
The people, all the people, citizens everyone,
All the nation and not the few.
The psychic imprint must not fade,
Our glorious future must be won.

To grasp the thistle, the nation must rise
Above the norm and seize the prize.

Ian Saint-Yves

In Denial

The TV displays, so many - so thin
It makes you quite angry where do you begin?
The fashion for fasting or the New Atkins diet
Not much of a chance of finding me try it.
I'm heavily boned, metabolic rates slow
As for where came the stomach - I really don't know.

It must be my age - I'm a grandmother too
It seems so unfair - but it's alright for you
Who eat what you like and never look back
While I'm too many potatoes put into a sack.
No bathroom scales - they'll never display
An accurate picture of what I should weigh
I've tried them before-those spiteful machines
I'd had severe trouble putting on jeans.

I've stopped eating chocolate this year for lent
The least I could do - to help me repent
But I didn't get slimmer-oh no not me
I'd found something else to take with my tea!
There's a wedding to go to in only three weeks
Oh how to get that figure that most of us seeks.

In the Chemist today I gasped with dismay
The digits display was too high
I reached for the door my poor heart was sore
As I left I said my goodbyes
The reality check was a pain in the neck
As I whispered 'no more weekend fry's'.

Margaret McLaughlin

Sinned

Your logic escapes me
While your disrespect rapes me
I tire of your games
And our entirely different aims
You hold me with your stare
I give away as much as I dare
I feel trapped and deceived
In a web I did not weave
My head has said no
But my heart has given in
Is falling for you such a mortal sin.

Lisa Rolls

Loving You

Loving you is like the fresh morning air,
Because it's for you my love I truly care,
Like the fresh mountain breeze,
Those velvety silken regal trees,
Your tender kiss and loving touch,
Makes me feel so very much,
From morning till night you always remain dear,
I convey my heartfelt love for you sincere,
Gazing into your serene dewy-eyes,
With your happy heart and hidden surprise,
From dawn till dusk I'll always love you,
With our united love blooming good and true,
Like golden waves in the sea of love
And silken wings of the treasured love dove,

Denise Hackett

Onwards And Upwards
(To Gordon and Harold)

Yes, well, it's another day
The papers, the news, the post
Arrive to challenge me
As if I hadn't challenge enough.

Then I look to the sun's first ray
Night fleeing like a martyred ghost
New strength flows to free me
From the dire fears of the 3 o'clock trough.

Yes! Today I will be me again
Choosing what I will think
Being my own self
Loving this one day and its life.

I will delight if the sun turns to rain
I will tell them I'm in the pink
I will be a cheeky mental elf
I will cut bad feelings with my mental knife.

Yet again! Each thought is a treasure
To have, to hold, to savour
From here I can see through so much
Life is rich to bring me such clarity of thought.

And just listen to music and its measure
Special people bringing me such grandeur
The whisper of art with its velvet touch
Today life gifts me with treasure un-bought.

Dear, dear close friends who give without reserve
Friends from the past, the now
The sun rises further and I clearly see
How much I have given that returns to me.

Joe Windsor

40 Wonderful Years

When I first saw you standing there,
and you held my hand,
I knew in an instant that you would understand,
You helped me cope, through the days
of bad and good,
And you showed your love to me
just like I knew you would.

You never let me down,
you were faithful to the end,
And to everyone around you,
you were their friend,
You gave them good advice,
whenever things went wrong,
And I hear people say to me now,
'You must be so strong'.

But now as I see you there so full of peace,
The pain that I saw edged on your face,
has now just ceased,
God came down to help you,
and to set you free,
And I know that deep within myself,
you had gone from me.

I hold a memory deep within my heart,
A beautiful memory, that must never part,
You meant the world to me,
and your love was so true,
But all I have left now,
are beautiful dreams of you.

Dreams that you came to me,
to let me know,
That throughout all our lives,
you really love me so,
You gave me wonderful memories
of such happy days,
And all your love came shining through
with your unselfish ways.

Barbara Holme

Teachers

The teachers went to sea on a maths book, they did
On a maths book they went to sea
Despite of all their pupils could say,
On a winter's morn, on a Thursday
On a maths book they went to sea,
And as the maths book got wetter and wetter,
The pupil's day got better and better
And all the pupils said
'We'll have a longer play time instead'
On a maths book they went to sea.

Sam Hyde

Contradictions Of Life

This world to me seems to be full of haunted souls drifting,
Floating through life searching for a place to anchor their hearts.
Somewhere safe where storms and rough seas
cannot hope to part them.
This world to me seems to be full of lonely hearts weeping,
Shedding tears because of the missing parts inside,
Waiting for the one who will end the misery
and guide them to happiness.

This world to me seems to be full
of restless minds tossing and turning,
Waiting for the calm that should eventually
consume all that is wrong,
And restore to order the mess that
had been there too long without cause.
This world to me seems to be full of hopeful faces wondering,
Gazing at their fate with joyful eyes,
Full of smiles for the happiness they feel will be there.

This world to me seems to be full of many happy couples sharing,
They seem to be loving, confiding and sincere,
And this becomes stronger as their years together roll by.
This world now to me seems to be full of promise,
Full of possibilities that everything will work out at last,
And that all that happened in our past
can be left there where it belongs.

This world now to me seems to be giving us a chance,
Time to fall in love over and over again,
Opportunities to build a solid base from where
we can then enjoy a happy life.
Yet this world to me seems to be full of contradictions, contrasts,
Like the bough in the wind, swaying one way and then the other,
Changing so often, so quickly, making me curious as to why I
bother to think about life at all.

But this life to me always seems to be unstoppable,
We are just pawns in her endless cycle of ups and downs,
Trying to survive as best we can before we eventually retire
to the ground and peace at last.

Tony Mitchell

How Twisted This World

How twisted this world in which we live.
A war's being fought against oppression.
Yet here am I, a normal day,
My temper tested in morning congestion.

The radio flashes news reports
A town is captured, lives are taken.
Then sports update, the soccer scores
The music begins; a pop sensation.

I sit & watch the TV news,
They broadcast live; each shot is shown.
A man approaches, his arms aloft
His fighting cause has cost his home.

Well groomed presenters discuss events
As images flash across the screen,
Reality of war a contradiction,
However real the pictures seem.

To a Hollywood movie, I must have tuned,
Stallone, Schwarzenegger or Clooney.
A familiar face will soon be seen
To save the world in time for tea.

But then the papers tell the story,
Across the page a woman's picture
Unanswered questions fill her eyes
My son is dead, where's his future?

So very real to a small proportion
This war affecting the world entire.
Retribution for unspeakable acts,
This is the reason your sons expire.

Peter Isgar

Babies

I know where babies come from,
Hidden under a bush.
A gooseberry one is the very best kind,
But any will do in a rush.

I know where babies come from.
They sit upon a shelf
In the doctor's surgery,
You can pick one for yourself.

I know where babies come from.
Stork brings them in his beak,
And if you're very nice to him
He'll let you take a peek.

I know where babies come from
I told my mum today.
Though why she's getting quite so fat
Is difficult to say!

Sharon A Jackson

72

Thoughts In Huntfield Garden

I sat in a beautiful garden
        and thought of the rose's fair
Ah! Soon I knew they'd be dying
        and the place of the rose's be bare.

I thought of the beautiful flowers
        All purple and golden and red
With sweet smelling pinks and white blossoms
        So soon to be withered and dead.

The trees were rustling around me
        Their foliage all fragrant and green
But Autumn had come with her mantle
        To spread o'er the beautiful scene.

The leaves that now are so verdant
        will soon be withered and sear
The garden that now is all blooming
        Will soon be silent and drear.

But Spring will come with its sunshine
        And strike the sundial again
And the dear sweet garden at Huntfield
        Will re-echo to beautiful strains.

Oh dear little birds singing blithely
        While building their nests in the trees
And roses just opening their petals
        Their fragrance to cast on the breeze.

Jane Reid

Our Special Bond

You're a great friend,
I hope our friendship never ends,
We have had our ups and downs,
But we always manage to sort,
All our troubles out,
You're always there for me,
When I need you the most,
You don't make fun out of me,
Because I'm not perfect,
Our friendship is so special to me,
Nothing can destroy the bond,
Between the two of us,
If we stick together,
We will over come,
 Every obstacle in our way,
I truly love you,
From the bottom of my heart,
Nothing and I mean nothing,
Will ever tear us apart.

Nina-sharina Jani

In Memory Of Elizabeth And Lucy

How can we know why they had to leave us?
What can we think that makes any sense?
Only that they came in order to love us,
To teach us that Love is why we exist.

Theirs is the voice of the blackbird in Springtime.
There they are, twinkling in each Winter star.
Though they were with us for only a short time,
We're not alone, as they haven't gone far.

Two little heads still look towards you.
Four little hands caress your face.
Two tender hearts reach out to love you.
Two rays of sun to comfort your days.

Judith Kelman

Growing Up

When born you cuddle your precious bundle.
Before you know it, off to school they'll trundle.
When they're young, down them sprouts and carrots you can bung.
Now burgers and pizza are much more fun!
Playing on swings used to bring so many joys.
Now computers and mobile phones are their new exciting toys!
Now they can open a door, that never shuts.
Laugh at your clothes and think your opinion sucks!
You try to teach them to learn.
Because to live, they'll have to earn.
When young on you they solely depend.
But one day, you'll be replaced by a special friend.
No matter what harsh words they may say.
They will always know, your love will stay.

Sharon Tregoning

Working Class

I am glad I was born of the working class.
Though to earn a crust I had to learn fast.
No silver spoon was stuck in my gob.
Or an upper class yob with no need of a job.
But the lessons I learnt have served me well.
Through years of war. Plus years of hell.
The working class. I am proud to say.
Are at their best on the darkest of days.
No better a class. No truer the friends.
Side by side we forged ahead.
From the working class came ninety percent
of the best in the world. And such fighting men.
But when the wars are won and the guns lie quiet.
It is back to the slog for a bed and a bite.
And widows weep in the lonely night for
those that lie in foreign graves.
With little thanks for the life they gave.
Where family is family. To have and to hold.
Boarding school for our kids? No, not at all.
Where there's no kiss or cuddle. Or a story that's told.
For a dorm may be full. Yet lonely and cold.
No mum or dad to tuck you in bed.
No one to calm you as you lay in dread of
the lightning and thunder and nightmares ahead.
I am proud to be of the working class.
Hard up. But helpful to others in need.
To cry when a pet must be put down to sleep.
We are the brawn and the brains.
And nothing has changed.
So the rest of you can kiss our arse.
And be grateful for us. The working class.

Den Johnson

Felicity

I'm a little fishing boat
Which chugs across Poole bay
I work with my good skipper
To earn his weekly pay.

Sometimes my 'catch' is heavy
At other times it's small
And then there are the bad times
When nothing's caught at all.

I have to feed the Poole folk
Who live in this fine town
With all food on rationing
I cannot let them down.

Today I'm chugging further
Than I have been before
To help the larger vessels
On some far distant shore.

Perhaps I will get tired
Doing this different work
So hope my fuel will last out
Until I reach Dunkirk.

I'm going to 'catch' brave soldiers
Who fought to save this land
I'll do my best to bring them
Back safe, to Poole (England).

Beryl King

Two Worlds

Distant lands in a small place
Two worlds in one
Two different likes
Two different views
Calm and peaceful
My land is
As I sit here
Far away
Listening, watching
I hear it, I see it
But I'm never part of it.

Helen L Smith

When The Days Get Colder

When the days get colder and
look like night time I see you in the fading
light. A body wrapped in blankets with feet
at one end and tiny face at the other. Folded
into the warmth of a blanket, dreaming maybe,
am I in your mind? It strikes me in this light how
blue everything looks, but your hair
will always be so dark and thick and heavy.
And I will never want to hold you more than
I do at this moment (do I say this too much?) but
I sit here, typing, trying to create a way to
remember this fading light moment before
you wake up and turn the lights on.

Alison May

Going Back To Cornwall

Going back to Cornwall,
We just can't get enough.
Where skies are full of colours,
And seas are sometimes rough.

There's always something new to see,
And places to explore!
Going back to Cornwall,
It draws me more and more.

The place that they call Roseland,
With a church that's called St. Just.
It's so beautiful and peaceful,
To visit is a must.

This little tranquil hidey hole,
That's by a sleepy bay.
Where local people lie to rest,
For ever and a day!

Going back to Cornwall,
Where the fishing boats prepare!
To cast their nets into the sea,
And catch whatever's there.

The little coloured cottages,
All standing in a row!
Fishermen returning home,
To harbour lights aglow.

There's Cornish pasties waiting,
With jam and cream for tea!
Going back to Cornwall,
Makes a Cornishman of me!

Susan Whitfield

Realisation

The small plop of the stone made tiny circles
That grew bigger, rounder
Encompassing the water
Capturing the moment
Sealed in vacuous pause.

Time stopped, hushed by the noiseless atmosphere
No insects buzzing, no birds wings flapping
No ripple of water caressing the pebbles
No warm sun teasing my fingers
Gone, as quick as a passing glance.

The warm toasting smell of the sun has vanished
The woody aromas of vegetation
And the sticky smell of tree sap
Fading forever
Floating off into the summer sky.

I want to taste again that fresh kick on my lips
Of the cold sharp water
Feeling it trickle down my body, making me shiver
The wild brambles no longer sweetening my breath
My mouth is neutralised and numb.

Over my head clouds are gathering
I have been isolated, selected
Encased in my bubble
Life goes past as I am in position
No sound, no feeling, no creature outside is aware
That my time has come.

Sandra E Lang

Just Up Ahead

See that old man,
That old man up ahead on the road,
Once upon a time he carried a chip
And then it became a load.

See that old man,
that old man ahead on the road,
once upon a time he had a wife,
he had children, that old man,
that old man, he had a life.

I know his story and it's a story you'd fear,
because a lot of it is down to beer
(or whiskey or whatever)
at the start he used to enjoy a drink,
he could drown his sorrows
and he didn't have to think.

Once upon a time he was a young man,
never thought enjoying a drink would
get him here.
Never thought a drink would lose him,
His wife, his children or his career.

Look at that old man,
Just ahead now on the road,
No! Look again at that old man,
look closely as you draw level on the road.

It's a very true saying 'there but for the
grace of God go I'.
A show of hands if you think I lie
So make your choice, we all have to try,
Walk with him or pass him by.

Oh please God; let me pass him by.

Muriel Maguire

Time Out

We climbed towards the mountains
As they towered to the sky.
Then we stopped to watch the buzzards
While they soared and glided by.
The air was sweet and scented,
Came the wafts of new-mown hay.
So we stopped and ate; decided
This would be our special day.

For we were both desk-weary
Driven hard a task to end;
Since it had to be completed
By a dead-line none could bend.
Hence the need to take some time off,
Get away from the office chores,
Have a time to raise the spirits
On this sparkling day outdoors.

We looked back the way we'd clambered
To the now small sheep below;
In fields the sunlight ambered,
Part of Nature's daytime show.
Then a drink, and upward walking
Till we reached the nearest peak;
Short of breath, with muscles aching.
Now at last had time to speak.

And we spoke of our enjoyment
At the pleasant break we'd shared,
Far from hours of dull enslavement
With a firm which seldom cared.
So we lazed there, in the sunshine,
Till the light began to wane.
Then we gathered our belongings;
And we started down again.

We were tired, warm and happy
When at last we reached our home
With a golden day to savour
In the darker days to come.

Jim Lawes

Mary's No Mug

Two people out on a Monday night
Both heading into town
One, Mary, smiling going to bingo
The other wore a frown.

For he was young and foolish
He needed another drug
He had a plan instilled in his head
A person he would mug.

So there was Mary, parking her car
Her thoughts were on the money
When from the dark she heard a voice
'Hand over your money honey'.

From the open window she saw a knife
It sparkled in the light
And in a flash her fist came up
She was ready for a fight.

She was frail and old, but she punched his face
The knife fell to the ground
She closed her eyes, ready for pain
But he left without a sound.

Who he was, she'll never know
She only can surmise
But she's eighty-three, just out for a game
And maybe win a prize.

Margaret McDonnell

Snow Reality

Snow falling like feathers from broken pillows.
The lamp catching their beauty
As they float, softly,
Carried along in the wind.

Then beautiful vision becomes harsh reality.
The feathers sting our faces
As we trudge, tensely,
Fighting to find shelter.

Back in the warmth, it still snows outside.
Peaceful Christmas scenes,
But, too late,
We know the broken truth.

Kate Mifrjobell

The Sun Will Smile

The sun will smile to the passers-bye
and thoughts of the rain will have run
away from the minds to be trampled by some
who believe winter has gone
and summer has come.

Thoughts of the people are happy again.
The flower's bowed heads no longer in shame
will lift and absorb.
New life is born and the children will come and play on the lawn.

The summer must end and the flowers will sleep.
Tired, slip quietly away.
To be nursed by the earth.
To be given re-birth,
Next year,
When summer is come.

Jennifer Miller

The Journey Of Life
(In musical terms)

Right from the beginning, try to be in tune
With your fellow men
Try not to hit the wrong note
Or you will be in the den!

Always try to harmonise
Its better than a solo part
'Though 'in unison' is sometimes needed
- So just take heart.

Discords may not always be avoided
As through life you go
But an even balance try to keep
And let things freely flow.

Crescendos make their loudest voice
For those who wish to hear
But diminuendos have their part to play
So softly and so clear.

All things have to be in tune
Made up of various parts
As long as we're all together
United, each one's heart.

Then the melody will display
How all things work for good
- Combination is the art
And for all time, this has stood.

The orchestration is complete
When each one makes the whole
Perfection surely then is reached
And this should be our goal.

Gillian Morgan

This Mirror

A mirror has been dropped
its smashed into a million pieces
all edges are sharp,
and will cause pain.
People walk over this mirror
they break the pieces
and make them even smaller.
This mirror is me
broken on the floor
someone dropped me,
and I smashed.
Here's a bit of my heart
oh and there's a piece of my soul
please stop standing on me
you're breaking me even more.
I will cause you pain
I will cause you suffering
that is why you will never love me.
I do this to all people
everyone I meet
I cause them pain
and then move on
to do the same again.
Yet they cause as much pain to me
standing on these pieces
these shards
that are me.
So please remember
when your trampling these bits
it was once a whole person
broken long ago.

Hannah Greaves

90

Truthful Advice

Everyone says that nothing will ever last
everything will end up in the past
all good things will be replaced by the new
all bad and evil will be renewed.

They say we only ever love once
and that love won't happen just by chance
it will come when we least expect it
and take hold so no one will suppress it.

So when it happens hold it tight
don't let it go
and put up a fight.
Take each moment and saturate with care
For this love thing is so special and rare.

Dawn Morris

There Is An Aching In My Heart

There is this aching in my heart that I just can't explain,
It is deep within my soul, this emptiness, the pain.
I want to hide; I want to stay low,
Please stop speaking now and let me go.
It's getting heavier now, that feeling inside,
I've tried to carry on and not just cried.
Woe is my pity, my shame and disgrace,
But I loved him then, and still I see his face.
He is in my mind, endless as the moon,
On this long lonely night caught in a loom.
I touch the softness of his pillow, yet it is as sharp as a knife,
How eerie this feels now he's gone from my life.
Each day I wake and know I am strong,
Until the sun shines in my eyes and I know I'm wrong.
Time is a great healer people say,
Oh give me time then, I pray.
Let me be an eagle and spread my wings out far,
I need to forget him and his wretched car!
I choose to fly and feel the wind in my face,
I want to do it all, but at my own pace.
I am fighting this plague called love and I will succeed,
For the first time, I am taking the lead.
I still see your image from time to time,
You are smaller now; I'm keeping you in line.
I suffer my moments, sadness and tears,
But life does go on through the years.
Each day I grow older, but wiser too,
Making sure I never encounter another you.
Yes you hurt me but you wounded yourself,
You will see there's more to life than wealth.
One day you will need me, be patient and see,
Oh how you're in trouble because you've set me free!
Now I move on with love in my hands,
For I am not alone as I walk along in the sands,
One day in the future another man may be,
But for now I'm happy it's just my mum and me.

Michelle Mountford

If You Knew Suzy Like We Know Suzy...
(With apologies to admirers of The Reverend Spooner)

I love Suzy Hayshine
So does Mo, my wife.
She brings us even closer
In the Autumn of our life.

We love Suzy Hayshine
She brings colour to our cheeks.
She makes our apples rosy
And nourishes our leeks.

We love Suzy Hayshine
She gives warmth without the heat.
She takes trousers from our legs
And puts sandals on our feet.

We love Suzy Hayshine
She encourages us to potter.
We make the most of every hour
On days when we have got her.

We love Suzy Hayshine
She is so calm and still.
She's better than Patsy Mitches
We just can't bear her chill.

Jim Ravenhill

Mo asked me if I'd seen the weather forecast on T.V. We laughed at my slip of the tongue when I had meant to reply 'hazy sunshine'. Suzy Hayshine has been a friend ever since.

Warm December

Will we walk in March, through the woods,
after snow has fallen 'crisp underfoot'
at some quiet part, so far undisturbed.
Will we quietly hold hands
or laugh gaily at our past
as friends walking?
Shall we speak of this moment of love
With a hand placed sweetly on face?
Will we talk of the last time
when we walked with another,
or will this walk the last one erase?

Georgia Weston

Vampires Have Feelings Too

I'm a vegetarian vampire
No blood shall pass my lips
I get my satisfaction from
The ketchup on my chips.

My teeth have gone all rotten
My fangs were far too long
'Fangs for the memory' has
Become my favourite song.

My family have all died out
The reason plain to see
Drinking blood of many maidens
Finished up with HIV.

My father was a werewolf
His genes he did endow
I used to be up half the night
But I'm quite cured noooooooooow!

No one wants a vampire
Especially one called Keith
'Cause I'm fat, bald and ugly
And only got false teeth.

Jeoff Newton

Stars

When I stay at my Nana's house,
We often look at the stars.
She knows the names of all of them,
She even knows which is Mars.

We sit close by the window,
We turn out all the lights,
The sky looks so exciting,
I love these magic nights.

One night was really special
We saw a shooting star,
We watched it zoom across the sky,
It hurtled off so far.

The thing that really puzzles me,
What happens in the day?
Where do the stars all go to?
Where do they hide away?

Christine Smith

Safe Ways

Satchmo plays his trumpet
It is late for Mac the knife.
He can't sing, but has a jazz delivery.
Jazz is classic, it doesn't date.
My times changed from standing still,
Now I still shop at Safeways on the Edgeware Road,
But nearer to Marble Arch. (The restaurants
Around Hyde Park aren't half bad and not as expensive
As you might think). As I walk home,
Looking in windows, it is raining.
Another Saturday night I have made piecemeal
From this broken time. It is safer -
To stick nearer the edge.
I can feel my life tick by
Second by second. The alarm bells ring
As I walk past St. Mary's Hospital.
Nothing is going to happen,
I tell myself. Nothing is going to happen,
That won't end here.
They hold the terrorists at Paddington Green.
Nothing is going to happen,
Out of the heart of west London.
We pray that nothing is going to happen,
And stick to Safeways on the Edgeware Road.

James Windsor

On A Day

On a day when emotions could be too much,
A day I had wanted to stay numb.
You came along and melted my icy façade;
You touched my heart.
On a day when I felt worthless,
Like I didn't fit.
You made me feel valued
And like I have a purpose.
On a day that I wasted and shut off,
You opened me up.
You made me feel how I thought I never would today.
Holding in the tears of not feeling 'I'm worth it'.
Holding in the pain but feeling it still,
But today you made it a joy to feel.
And once the pain subsides there can only be happiness.

Jessica Warren

I Miss You Very Much

How I miss the smell of your hair and skin,
And the feeling of your touch,
Mum and Dad, I miss you both so very much,
Crying doesn't take away the pain anymore,
And nothing I do here seems the same,
Why did you go and leave me,
Sometimes I feel so alone and I just cry and cry,
And sit and scream WHY?
I know you had to go, you couldn't stay,
But I know we will be together some day,
One day, just not yet, as much as I miss you,
I still have too much to do,
But when my body needs a good rest,
When I am resting I will think of you both, as you were the best,
I just wish for just one day, I could see you again,
As I know you are watching me, I just want it to be true,
If you're here somewhere around, please would you,
Make a noise or sound, just so I know you're really around,
Dad and Mum, it's a long time since you went away from me,
And I miss you both, as you can see,
I sit and talk to your picture on the wall,
And Mum and Dad I love you lots,
Dad I miss and love you most of all,
You both listened to me when I was in pain,
And we loved it when you came to our house, even in the rain.
So don't forget me, I won't you,
How could I, you know my love for you both is true,
While you are both in Heaven having a rest
Please look over me, my darlings and God bless.

Margaret Wright

The Call Of The Drum

(A Launching Of The 'Zetland' At Redcar in 1803)

Nature's forces are in conflict tonight
Raging storm, thunder claps, lightning's blinding light,
Faintly a tap, tap, tapping supersedes nature's might.

'Tis the insistent call of the snare drum
Tum ti tum, titi tum, tum tit tum
Tum ti tum, titi tum, tum tit tum.

Come along, bonnie lads, come along!
We need you bonnie lads, come along!
To bend an oar, bonnie lads, come along!

Bobbing lanterns, reflecting in bull's eye window pane
Like fireflies, dancing down Smithies Lane
Glinting on the cobbles, saturated with rain.

Doors slamming, excitement mounting, running feet
Boots pounding down narrow winding cobbled street
Responding to the snare drummers urgent beat.

'Five for the white, five on the blue
Two on steers, five to complete the crew
Come on bonnie lads, we're relying on you.'

Launching crew rush her down the beach
Thro' the surf, float her out of reach
Of crashing waves, dipping oars pull to the 'Mary Leach'.
Eighty years, 'Zetland' answered the call of the drum
Five hundred souls saved with her total sum,
On a stormy night, yet, echoes the call of the drum
Tum ti tum, titi tum, tum tit tum,
Bend an oar, bonnie lads, come along!

Ghostly echoes of a bye gone age,
Tum ti tum, titi tum, tum tit tum,
Tum ti tum, titi tum, tum tit tum,
We need you, bonnie lads, come along.
The call to the 'Zetland' on a snare drum.

A Quinn

Amber Eyes

He holds the glass up to the light,
the amber liquid shining bright,
that's brewed by man for mans delight.
Each night he sits there at the bar,
the landlord filling up his jar,
his conversation tends to bore,
the barmaids heard it all before,
and when its time they close the door,
but he stays on for just one more,
then staggers home its not too far,
there was a time he owned a car,
a loving wife that waited home,
but now he lives there all alone.
His memories are very blurred,
one vivid moment when he swerved,
one picture of his pretty wife,
that night he crashed and took her life.
His aching heart is full of pain,
and amber liquid dulls his brain,
an empty life now full of shame.
He only has himself to blame,
If time could turn back just one year,
He wouldn't touch a drop that's clear.
He'd hold his sweetheart in the night
and kiss her amber eyes so bright.

Estella Swann

Final Stage

You're filling me with so much rage,
With out you even here.
You're trapping me in your steel cage,
You're invoking all my fear.

My mind of love, fear and hate,
My body filled with blood.
A mind lost and dead, was fate.
A body open wide, red flood.

Blood slowly dripping down my fingers,
Painting walls with a shout.
A deep red fist still lingers,
Red rivers, cold, in drought.

Chris Purdy

Good And Bad News

Your son hasn't been late for school Mister Head
For one whole year said strange Miss Red
That's the good news you see
Now the bad news dearie
It's because he's played truant for the whole year she said!

Joan M Wylde

The Highway Man

Lurking in the shadows in the fading light of day.
Furtively he watches before pouncing on his prey.
No violence has he ever used as he robs them of their wealth.
This charismatic fellow with lots of charm and stealth.
Some say there are many highway men of every shape and size.
But I know there is only one and he is a master of disguise.
Alert and ever watchful as he journeys to his home.
Making sure he's not been followed making sure that he's alone.
In the privacy of his dwellings he produces a canvas bag.
A crooked smile curves his lips as he fingers his stolen swag.
Who would think this country squire with property so grand.
Would be the notorious highwayman sought throughout the land.
Will he ever be caught I wonder? Only time will tell.
For he is crafty and elusive like the scarlet pimpernel.

Margaret Power Burnip

The Lost City

A hardly there breeze
Honeyed fragrance on the air
Hovers the bee's wing.

Dragonfly hanging
Over stagnant water still
It waits suspended.

Spiders are weaving
Webs of fantasy that lure
Fragile threads to death.

Here in Babylon
The smell of burning almonds
Pervading choked air.

The machine hovers
Over head it waits to strike
Death is imminent.

Politicians weave
Explanations left wanting
Of why we are here.

When the machine strikes
Life is obliterated
As the bees sting burns.

Marjorie Nye

La Symphonia De La Picadores

Cervantes shouted from the highway, 'Hey',
the dust storm rose, tall wild grey rose,
growing on horizons line.
Papyrus scrolls talking to the plains,
the roaring plains España,
ancient and brittle, wise and harsh,
the roaring plains España.
The riders in black, dustedcoveredblack,
ride bulls like they were birds,
tame the knights insignificant, let only to watch the herd,
pass them by...... pass them by....... pass them by.
With their thunder they take away,
with their enormity they retrieve,
with their blackness mass, storm rolling task,
ripple the hearts of men.
The bulls rode hard that day.
Covering all of Spain.
No man was left to speak.
When the bulls rode hard that day.
Covering all of Europe.
Great swaths of land cut through.
Bull riders symphony in black.
In black and riding true.

Graeme Robbins

Rainbow

Within a rainbow I do so live,
colours around me this to give,
Many the colours dark and so light,
they are there abundant in my sight,
My favourite it is that of the green,
its many shades, some with a sheen,
Our world then so prettily dressed,
with shades of colour intimately caressed,
Weaving in and out in life's dream,
such wonderful colours to be seen,
Colours to brighten many the day,
brings much love and peace our said way,
The rose of red, we all this do know,
love it brings where ere it may go,
The marigold so brilliant and bright,
too many the eye such a beautiful sight,
The uplift of these in a man's heart,
many more, they all take part,
Flowers are there, their glory to be,
all dressed in colour for us to see,
The sky, this look upwards for us to see,
many the changes and patterns for you and me,
Colours are the many in and around,
in them a beauty for to be found,
Our world so giving in this of its light,
even its darkness found many spectacular a sight,
The stars and that of our own moon,
bringing all it shines on its own plume,
The colours of our world so many to see,
just like the rainbow there to always be.

June Davis

Nature

Come walk with me and take my hand.
To stroll through natures wondrous woodland,
We always look but sometimes don't see
The beauty of nature that's there
For you and for me.

Clusters of flowers their heads held high
Seeking the suns warmth from the clear blue sky,
So many colours yellow, pinks and blue
Drink each gentle drop of early morning dew,
Look all around when you walk through the glades
A canvas of colours of so many shades,
Flowers some big and some that are small
Each with its own beauty somehow stands tall.

Trees stand like sculptures, their branches so tall
Still have a kind of beauty when their leaves start to fall,
A carpet of leaves spread softly on the ground
Brown, golden colours are often abound.

When winter comes snow spreads on the ground
Its wildlife will sleep not making a sound.
Yet snowdrops appear peeping out of the frost
Even in winter its beauties not lost.

Don't take for granted this awesome scene
Array of colours mixed with brown and green.
Its breathtaking beauty as each season unfolds
The wonder of nature is one to behold.
So take sometime out to stop, look and see
What nature provided its there and its free.

Mary Murray

Fun For All

Did you ever visit a charity fayre?
See all the stalls with their goods displayed there.
Tombola, and bric a brac. Bottles and toys,
Plenty for everyone, mums, dads, girls and boys.
Cakes by the dozen, and sandwiches too.
Stalls full of all sorts, with plenty to do.

Try your luck on the raffle, great prizes to win.
You could win a clock, or biscuits with tin.
Whatever you choose to spend your money on,
And whether on games you have lost, or you've won
You'll return home feeling happy you've been,
Thinking of all you have bought and have seen.

A rabbit with suitcase, or pig with a slot,
Blue teddy, pink tortoise and plant in a pot.
A battered old book, once so cherished, well read,
To some lucky child as he's tucked up in bed.
And did you notice, alone in a corner
A photo of Grandma, whose family still mourn her?

The clothes stall with trousers, coats, bonnets and such.
Will provide something for all, and they don't cost much
No need to go hungry, there's refreshments too.
Tea, coffee and biscuits, and not a long queue.
The raffle is drawn, just before close.
Are you winners, or losers? Nobody knows.

Shirley Small

Daydreams

Tousled golden curls
Bright eyes full of wonder,
Riding on her rocking horse
        Dreaming,
Of her birthdays and school friends
Holidays and Christmas,
Happy childhood daydreams.

Trendy clothes and hairstyle
Starry eyes full of wishes,
Listening to her radio
        Dreaming
Of pop stars and discos,
Parties and boyfriends,
Romantic teenage daydreams.

Hair still in rollers,
Tired eyes full of worries,
Washing up dirty dishes
        Dreaming
Of exotic faraway places,
Lazy, peaceful sun-filled days
Wistful secret daydreams.

Silver haired old lady
Faded eyes full of wisdom,
Sitting alone on a park bench
        Dreaming
Of a young carefree girl
Holding hands with her true love
Bitter sweet daydreams.

Ruth Singlehurst

Soaring High

As I walk along I do not think
I stroll along using instinct
It was like that, early that morning
When the call came

I was not depressed
I did not thinking at all
I just drove, on autopilot
Time stood still

I was there before I left
The house was warm
The house was calm.
I was home.

That time had come
The time for passing, for moving on
It was not my time
It was time for the giver of life.

I still felt no pain, I felt nothing
I moved into place, on the left.
And waited for the end.
Waiting for the passing.

I was calm, I was patient
When that moment came
The pain had come
Then that moment stood still.

Slow motion a life released
The soul set free
On wards and up wards
Soaring high.

With that it was over
With that it was beginning
The pain was over for the giver
And the pain was just beginning for me.

Andrew Philpott

No Promised Land

You work hard all your life
You work hard and pray
You'll get your reward
Come judgement day
Well that's what they tell you
And think you don't understand
There's no religion, no promised land.

You live your life full
Be honest and true
You don't need no preacher
Telling you what to do
You're not going to hell
Get up make a stand
There's no religion, no promised land.

Million's have died
In the name of the Lord
From hunger to murder
Can you tell me what for?
Why can't He stop it
With a wave of his hand?
There's no religion, no promised land.

You worship in fear
While hungry kid's die
But there'll be no lightning
Coming down from the sky
If I was famous
This might be banned
There's no religion, no promised land.

Alan Unsworth

Beauty, Sound And Colour

Voices singing to the wind from whence the echoes lie
A leaf armada in a stream goes gently floating by
A thousand droplets cling together
And wind their downward course
Through greens and browns and country towns
To leave behind their source
A calling lark, a sound so splendid carries on the air
Little children playing freely having not a care
The world's a garden, decked in colour, formed by an artist's hand
To live in peace with those we love, now wouldn't that be grand
Fast falls the night but beauty doesn't die
A million stars like tiny candles brighten up the sky
Both dark and light have things to thrill us
Keep watch and be amazed
For all this beauty; sound and colour
Our lord god must be praised.

Bob Newell

Iced-tooth

Iced-tooth sharp air
sets the neck angled
ink skywards as
points of distant
light remind us
who we once were.
Pavement, still shiny
rain wet dampens
foot echoes towards the
pub where juke-vodkaed
roll-up beered and wine-operaed
souls search for the moment.
The pin-point knife-edge
moment
when the look is returned as sure
as gravity itself.
The look that says
all will be reciprocated
now, tomorrow and forever.
And, in that millisecond
of recognition
a number of things
might happen.
But even if the best
becomes temporarily real,
the duty of our
contracts
leads us back tied kicking
and gagged screaming
to a life where
each clause is defined
to exclude
the possibility of passion,

Nick Nakorn

For You

You are the moon
You are the sun
You are the sky up above
You are the one who lives forever
You are the one that I love
You are my strength
You are my weakness
You are all of my blood
You are the one that is loving
You are the one that is good
You are the sea
You are the ocean
You are the eyes in my head
You are all that I feel
You are all that I dread.

You are the one that I belong to
You give me hope
You give me light
You give me understanding
You make me feel
You make me see
You make me want and want for more
You make me happy not sad
You take but in return you give
You make me love and not to hate
You know that it's true
You know that it's fact
You know that it's fate.

You are all of life's beautiful things.

You are the one
You are no other
You are special
You are my lover.

Ian Sneyd

117

The Moon

Bright shining stars in a dark velvet sky
Tailed comets through the atmosphere fly
The silvery light of the moon's pale beams
Coldly illuminates earth and it seems
The countryside has come to life
An owl swoops silently over his prey
Unblinking eyes distinguish night from day
Small creatures rustle on the wood's leafy floor
Small squeaky sounds, bats flitting ever lower
As Luna strolls through the heavens
She spreads her cloak wider while mortals sleep
Reflecting herself in the still waters deep
Greeting Orion who hunts the night sky
Bending her knee as shooting stars pass by
Till the first light of a brand new day.

Jeanette Niven

Autumn Leaves

Gold and yellow tumbling leaves,
Tap dance along the ground with ease.
They give a performance that looks inspired
Prompted simply by the unseen breeze!

Stop a while and watch the show,
Created by these gymnastics dancers.
The oak leaves look like little people
Dressed up in suits of vivid colour.

They entertain with movement and sound.
A pirouette, a somersault, a rustling dance.
Others surround them with earnest clapping.
Suddenly they go quiet, as if in a trance.

Once the proud branches held them high.
They gave us a spectacle of colour that thrilled the eye.
Colours of ochre, sienna, magenta and gold.
They are every Autumn season's magnificent show!

Eventually they have to leave their dizzy heights
And descend to the ground like little parachutes.
There they partner the wind for their final fling.
Finally resting as carpet, under the unclothed trees.

Linda Whiteley

Echoes Of The Seaside

The seaside - refreshed by the sun,
day-trippers everywhere,
summer has begun!

Buckets and spades, rockpools and sand,
ice-cream and doughnuts,
everything to hand.

Amusement arcades, 40p rides,
deckchairs on the beach -
be careful of the tides!

Look out to sea,
speedboats in a race -
walks along the pier at a leisurely pace.

Trampoline jumping on the beach,
bouncy castles - at £1 each!

Trouser legs rolled up,
paddling in the sea -
fish and chips with a cup of tea!

Happy days are here to stay,
enjoy yourself and have a nice day!

Jeanie Roach

The Boy In The Picture

Colourless and scorn,
in the picture he sits.
Half a boy complete,
twisted without a mind.
He has no way to live,
no way to love.
The things that we must endure,
he can only wish to have.
But he can only look out at us...
feeling sad.
His face is blurred,
but he has not been drawn bad.
With perfection, to the touch,
he has been made in pain.
Unable to feel or sense,
because he has been forced this way.

The boy in the picture.

Scott Sinfield

The Lover's Turmoil

One little request
and he's at her behest-
with one single phone call.

He's torn - but
inexplicably drawn-
like a moth to a flame.

She aims to please
making him at ease-
giving infinite pleasure.

He cannot desist,
and cannot resist
like metal to a magnet.

Her adulation,
and his justification
help to give him solace.

But his wife's previous rejection
and his self-recrimination
are emotions to plague him.

He dreads turning to stone,
finally living alone
without a loving partner.

She's not ideal,
but has magnetic appeal
which fills an empty void.

She has cast her spell
but who can tell
the endurance of these emotions?

His rose coloured specs are still so strong
but for just how long
will they hold their power?

Beryl Stone

For An Anger Misplaced

This broken thing,
Spilt on the streets,
For an anger badly misplaced.

I won't judge
And you shan't judge
And they can't be judged
For an anger sadly misplaced.

Richard Ellis